Being 20-Something

A compass for navigating early adult life

OKEZI OBRUTU

Being 20-Something

Copyright © 2022 **Okezi Obrutu**

A catalogue copy of this book is available at the National Library of Nigeria.

ISBN (Paperback): **978-978-791-760-2**

Genre: Self-help, Personal Development, Personal Success

Unless otherwise indicated, all Scripture quotations are taken from the Holy Bible, New Living Translation, copyright © 1996, 2004, 2007 by Tyndale House Foundation. Used by permission of Tyndale House Publishers, Inc., Carol Stream, IL 60188. All rights reserved.
Scriptures are taken from the New King James Version®. Copyright © 1982 by Thomas Nelson, Inc. Used by permission. All rights reserved.

While the author has made every effort to provide accurate Internet addresses at the time of publication, neither the author nor the publisher assumes any responsibility for 3rd party content, errors, or for changes that occur after publication.

Cover Design
Funmi Okonta

Edited by
Divadesign Resource Company
(DIVABYDESIGNRC)

All correspondence should be addressed to...
okezi.ob@gmail.com
www.okeziob.com

Published and printed in Nigeria by

+2348083942528, +2348140131255
#13, Gbajabiamila Street, off Camp Davies Road, Ayobo, Lagos, Nigeria
www.valuepluspublishingng.com.ng

For my sister, Kome

You already know the full story. I hope this book helps to make my life's exposures, experiences and learnings count for yours, and many others.

Prologue

D URING MY FIRST YEAR AT UNIVERSITY, I HAD AN unwelcome introduction to the reality that life, as it were, had changed.

There had been rumours that May 27 would not be a holiday, but I refused to believe because May 27 (aka Children's Day) had been a standard holiday for students as far back as I could remember. Surely if there was a change to something so significant, there would have been an official announcement, right? Well, it turned out that I was wrong.

The rumours were true, and there was no official announcement. To cap it all, I had a really boring lab session to attend that day. I was mad at the entire situation and probably more upset at the fact that I wasn't pre-informed than about the lack of a holiday. Worse still, there was no one to direct my mumbled emotions toward, so I was left to seethe all by myself.

In hindsight, I see how that situation was a shadowed forecast of this adulting life with its barrage of expectations and no pre-information or *how-to* manual. I should have known to reserve my emotions for the bigger surprises that were ahead!

Foreword

IN 2020, IN THE THICK OF THE COVID-19 PANDEMIC, I met Okezi virtually and it was my absolute pleasure to coach her in discovering, expressing, and maximising her God-given talents. She is extremely talented in analysing situations, creating systems & processes for them, and spotting growth areas in others to help them develop; hence it came as no surprise to me when she mentioned the purpose of this book.

As I read through, Okezi's desire to use her talents, skills, and experiences to contribute to the lives of others is clearly seen in a very practical and valuable way. Each chapter of the book is filled with lots of wisdom. It also has very clear and concise ways for the reader to navigate each key area discussed and ends with very useful Personal Reflection Questions that create a system for the reader to reflect and progress. I am excited to see this book serve as a great guide that positively impacts the lives of those who read it.

Foluso Gbadamosi

Executive Director, Junior Achievement Nigeria.
Transformation Coach (Gallup Certified Strengths Coach)

Contents

Introduction

THE EARLY YEARS OF ADULTING COULD FEEL LIKE being in the shoes of a 5-year-old who somehow wins the lottery. Although this would be *really good* news, it would also be *really BIG* news! This child who can now afford all the good things of life and live large can just as easily ruin his/her life by making certain decisions that affluence affords him/her.

Just like this child, it's easy to feel like you're a full-time adult with all the associated freebies e.g., life on your own terms (let's pretend it really is, haha!). These are the good parts - You own the cash, set the curfew, control the keys and TV remote because you now live alone!

The *BIG* part is this – you are completely responsible now; for the bills, showing up on time, getting the job done, keeping the doors locked. You are responsible for the full-time consequences of your decisions. While parents, siblings, and friends may felicitate with you occasionally, perhaps they even try to convince you to follow what they believe is the *right path*, it still cannot take away the fact that you have become the highest stakeholder in this gain or blame game.

BEING 20-SOMETHING is a metaphor I coined for this phase of life. It is the phase of baptism into adulthood. While this may occur earlier than age-20 for some or later than age-29 for others, most people encounter it within this age range.

As important as this phase is for the rest of our lives, nothing quite prepares most people for the reality of this season. While a few are lucky to have parental advice, early life experiences or witnessed events in the life of others as preparatory lessons, many of us arrive at adulthood essentially unprepared.

This lack of preparation can easily cause unnecessary pain and damage depending on whether it takes weeks, months, or years to recognize and address it. On a smaller scale, arriving unprepared translates to confusion and frustration which I have often heard expressed as: "I want to go back". This I have at some point said myself.

However, since we know that the days, we have on this earth are short and a gift from God, it is important that we embrace adulthood as the gift it truly is. This realisation should also drive us to search for wisdom to make the best of this phase. We really should join the ancient Psalmist to pray, "So teach us to number our days, that we may apply our hearts to wisdom".

> *"Wisdom is key to making our days count."*

In the pages of this book, I will share the wisdom that I have gained from Scriptures, personal experiences, books, courses, reflections, and conversations with friends, to help you navigate this transition to adult life.

I discuss seven core themes which stand out as cornerstone areas. These will be vital as you design your life to reach for the greatness that is already a seed within you.

I encourage you to find the time to document your learnings and reflections as you go along. More so, I hope you share them with a friend or two. Please make it a priority to write out your answers to the reflection questions for each chapter before moving on to the next, so that you can build on this foundation in the days ahead.

My prayer is that your interaction with this book will help you grow and supply you with wisdom and strength to thrive through this first decade of adulthood and beyond.

"So, teach us to number our days, that we may apply our hearts to wisdom."

PSALM 90:12 NKJV

Identity

REALLY, WHO AM I?

I REALLY LOVE HANGING OUT WITH CHILDREN. HOW they can be so beautiful and carefree, yet potentially dangerous, warms my adult heart a lot. Just ask a parent whose kids have gotten themselves stuck under furniture. Beyond warming my heart though, I enjoy watching children translate their thoughts into words without hesitation. Find yourself children who feel like they are in a safe space and you're certain to hear them blurt out whatever is on their mind, often in the form of questions. Actually, in the form of a lot of questions.

In a way, we are all like children with lingering questions, although as we grow, we are socialised to become less spontaneous with asking. For as long as we are unable to find satisfactory answers, we live with this curiosity that often seeps through one way or another. One of the big questions that we hardly ever outgrow is the question of *identity*. Beginning as children, we wonder who we are and where we are from. These queries herald our search for significance and grow with us when left unanswered. I know a few people were fortunate enough to get a person or resource in their childhood that provided adequate and satisfactory answers. These folks typically start early with that advantage, and it makes them so confident that they almost come across as being cocky.

Unlike the lucky few, a majority are saddled with the responsibility of figuring out who and whose they are by themselves. This creates an identity gap that needs to be fixed, as it can adversely affect the foundations on which these individuals stand as they interact with the world. This fix is even more vital for young adults, as adulthood is well-poised to shake foundations and bring to the fore questions about origin and identity that were never considered. How then do we address this? That is exactly the point of this chapter.

First, Where Does a Sense of Identity Come From?

According to verywellmind.com, identity is *"an overarching sense and view of oneself."* Cambridge dictionary defines it as *"a person's name and other facts about who they are,"* while Oxford Languages defines it as *"the fact of being who or what a person or thing is."* Another definition by YourDictionary.com is *"who you are, the way you think about yourself, the way you are viewed by the world and the characteristics that define you."*

Drawing from the above, my preferred definition of identity is *"…an individual's most compelling description of themselves, to themselves."*

The way we see ourselves through our own lens in the absence of other people's influences ultimately determines our sense of identity. While the above definitions make it clear that the concept of identity is complex and dynamic, we know that identity forms the basis of how each of us relates with ourselves and how we present ourselves to others. For example, someone who thinks they are awesome is likely to engage in positive self-talk which seeps into how they present themselves as they relate with other people.

> *"Identity is an individual's most compelling description of themselves, to themselves."*

On the other hand, a person who thinks of themselves as trash goes on to present that vibe to others and then wonders why they are consistently treated in a certain way.

A sense of identity can evolve over time based on a combination of nature and nurture. Having been a Sunday School teacher for many years, I have witnessed quite often the reality of nature-born identity. Quite frequently, I encounter a 3-year-old who is convinced that she is the leader of the team and consequently, everyone needs to do as she says. At this age, it is not likely that this sense of identity is due to nurture, because 3-year-olds are not yet actively learning about who they are in relation to others. As a matter of fact, the same child in another few years may become plagued by a less certain sense of themselves that could result from their environmental influences. On the other hand, a nurtured sense of identity evolves from upbringing, life experiences, media exposure and personal reactions to life events. In this case, people pick up and retain lessons about who they are from their interactions with external influences. A good example is this:

From an early age, I had thought that I was ugly. While I cannot trace this sense of identity to a specific event, I know that at the age of 9 when I set out for secondary school, I was convinced about this view of myself. This influenced how I saw myself and interacted with others in the context of a large boarding school with over 2000 students. However, as I interacted with other students, I noticed they often made comments about how beautiful I was.

At first, I did not pay any attention to this. I felt that these comments were simply patronising and I was not going to fool myself by taking any inauthentic words seriously. Well, I happened to change schools after my first year and at my new school, people still made comments about me being beautiful. It was at this point that I started to make allowance in my mind for the possibility that I was not ugly, and I eventually reconciled myself to a sense of identity that includes 'beautiful'.

In this case, my sense of identity was positively nurtured by the external environment, but this is not always so. As a matter of fact, transitioning to adulthood will more likely provide a less-than positive nurture to your identity especially with the new demands placed on you, the false sense of competition around, and the all-too-familiar feeling of inadequacy that takes free residence in many unsuspecting minds. This places even more responsibility on an individual to nurture their sense of identity deliberately and positively for the sake of their own mental health, their life pursuits, and the far-reaching effects on other aspects of life.

I believe that there are two components to consider when thinking about a healthy identity:

1. Foundational Identity

Your foundational identity is related to a sense of who you are which is irrespective of circumstance or position. For example, I now see myself as inherently beautiful and valuable no matter where I am, who I am with, or what is happening per time. I have grown into this confidence based on a conviction about how I arrived at this place and time called earth, and my certainty about what the Creator of this Universe that I occupy thinks about me. I know for sure that when God saw all that He had created, He called it *good*, therefore, I believe I am *good*.

Let us further explore this component based on the question, "who am I?"

There are two simple answers to this question that set you up for success in figuring out your identity. The first is this – *I am a created being.*

It is no news that humans, and indeed all of creation did not appear here by accident or by some *big bang,* neither did we show up on our own terms. The science of reproduction helps us understand that the chances of each of us being here are so slim that for any of us to have made it here, there definitely was an orchestrator and intention at work. The recognition of the fact that we are created does several things to us.

First, it frees us to understand that we are inherently valuable because someone far more powerful than us thought so. Next, it humbles us with the realisation that the value we have was bestowed on us. This applies to every single human irrespective of age, gender, colour, income, educational attainment and whatever else we add to the list. In addition, it implies that we are not quite capable or worthy of *"un-bestowing"* this honour upon ourselves. Consequently, an acceptance of your created reality positions you to understand and accept that there is something special about you.

Knowing that you were created also drives a realisation that your being here is not accidental. As a matter of fact, if you are still here, after all these years – despite the odds – it makes sense to consider (and agree) that there is a purpose your presence is intended to serve. Taking all these factors into consideration allows you to embrace yourself and accept that you are a significant "somebody", to at least "one body". And hey – it is this one person that counts the most, so why the stress?

The other answer that sets you up for a grounded identity is this – *I am loved and enough*. How do I know this? The Bible clearly tells us that God sent His Son, Jesus, to die because He *so* loved the world. In case you forgot, it was His *only* Son, and He did that long before you cared the least bit about Him.

Also, He is doing all He can today to get your attention – I know that for sure because this book found its way into your hands. If you believe in God and the message of Jesus, my friend, there is no excuse at all in the world to make you feel unloved. Even if you do not, this still applies to you, because last I checked, you are a human in the world. What more proof do you need to affirm that you are loved, special and important?

Take a moment to reflect on this truth – "You were created, and your Creator calls you good!" As you reflect, incorporate this into your internal dialogue with yourself until you are convinced about it. This will set you on your way to becoming a grounded individual who is better prepared to interact with life as a *twenty-something*.

Be mindful that settling this truth in your mind does not mean that you will not have doubts along the way, but it will make it easier to have answers beneath the surface that pop right into your consciousness on the day of need.

2. Evolutional Identity

Your evolutional identity is your sense of self that takes its shape or form depending on a position you occupy or a challenge you are faced with. This component of identity likely evolves as you progress in life and take on new roles from time to time e.g., as an employee at a new job, a new wife or husband, parent, aunt, or uncle, etc.

At a new job, this could be related to how you think of yourself based on the spoken or unspoken encouragement or criticism you get after handing in your first deliverable. For a new mom, this could be centred around your thoughts and feelings about being great or terrible at what you do as you navigate the uncharted waters of motherhood.

While this component of identity appears to be more volatile, it is still important to pay attention and ground yourself firmly on this side. This is even more relevant because *the way you see yourself has direct implications on your performance and experiences in these roles.* Since you will eventually spend the bulk of your time — and life — in these positions, it is only reasonable to set yourself up for the best possible experience.

I believe that issues related to this component of identity typically rest on the premise of: Capability, Competence and Capacity; therefore, building a solid foundation demands answering questions about these concepts beforehand. These questions generally apply across the board, regardless of the specific situation or role.

One of the first questions that may plague you as you take on a new responsibility is this – "Am I capable?" which can be translated as, "Can I really do this?" My answer is, "Yes, you can!". Though I haven't met you, I can tell you why I am certain.

Remember when you first started to walk and how many times you stumbled and fell? Okay, maybe you do not remember, but I am sure someone in your life does, and you should ask them. However, most people overcame that initial struggle and eventually learned to walk except if there was a physical or physiological limitation. We overcame many of the things we struggled with as kids because we kept on trying and grew our capacity.

As an adult, you can lean on this history and take it as evidence that you can. You really can do whatever you set your mind to, even if it takes a while to manifest competence. You are capable and able to fill this role and carry out its demands. Let this sink in and then carry it within as an aspect of your identity. You can if you will!

Another question that often fuels a shaky sense of self is "What if I ruin this?" And to this, my response is – there is no such thing! You will never know if you don't try and even if you ruined it, I promise you won't be the first… or last. All you will have to do would be to try again until you eventually master it.

Think about this – if nobody did anything till they were perfect at it, nothing would ever get done and perfection would be a fantasy. Mastery and perfection happen by continuous practice.

A healthy sense of identity hinges on your recognition and acceptance of your imperfections not as limitations, but as opportunities for growth. Based on this recognition, you can put in the tenacity and humility to get from point A (novice) to point B (professional). Because it is a long journey, this foundation is important to help you persevere to perfection in whatever it is you find yourself doing, whether that's being a professional, spouse, parent, or regular adult (if there's any such thing, lol).

> *The fact that you make a mistake today says nothing about how adept you will be tomorrow, so do not let it make you feel less than you are!*

Remember, you are not big, strong, or qualified enough to ruin God's plans for your life, you only need to build your capability to pursue His plans.

A final question I will consider is one that asks, "Do I really deserve this?" or "Should I really be here?" You probably know my answer already, but I will reiterate – Of course, you do! You deserve every good thing that comes your way, and you belong at every table where you choose to show up.

The impostor syndrome has been recognized for what it is: *an individual's irrational fear that they are not competent enough to occupy their place at a table, even though they put in legitimate effort to get there.*[1]

Even if it feels like you did not do enough work to get there, accepting your place is a good way to show gratitude to whoever or whatever that made it happen for you. Come on, how random does chance get to put someone like you in a seat that gives you the opportunity to contribute to something of value? And except this is not a place you want to be, I encourage you to sit tight in that seat and do what is required of you in that place.

> **You are worthy of favour and deserving of every good that comes your way!**

Guess what the Scriptures tell me?

"A man can receive nothing except it be given him from heaven"

JOHN 3:27 NKJV

God gave you this grace, and it would please Him for you to own it and do your best with it.

---

[1] *Langford, J and Clance PR. The Impostor Phenomenon: Recent Research Findings Regarding Dynamics, Personality and Family Patterns and Their Implications for Treatment. Psychotherapy. Vol 30(3).*

Having explored both the foundational and evolutional components of identity, it is important to note that neither of them exists in a silo. Because they are interdependent, they both deserve attention, although the balance may tilt in different seasons of life.

For example, what you see yourself as on a constant basis is likely to influence how you think of yourself when you face a new situation. Likewise, your perception of yourself in evolving situations can produce results that in turn influence your constant perception of yourself i.e., your foundational identity. This underscores the need to be deliberate about fortifying yourself on both fronts.

How Do I Develop a Healthy Sense of Identity?

To start your journey to a healthier sense of identity, you need to begin with an honest evaluation of your current state.

The amount of work you need to do will depend on where you are starting from, and it is a process that will require continuous investments over time. The following points offer a handle to get started with:

✓ Start by identifying what your prevailing sense of identity is today. What do you most often *tell yourself about yourself* when you are *by yourself?*

What do you think is your nature, and what factors have nurtured you, or what have you nurtured up to this point? Take time to think about this thoroughly until you get to the underlying drivers of the different things you believe about yourself.

✓ Hold the ideas you find from your inquiry against the ideas and scripture references presented so far, in this chapter, and reason with them until you are convinced about what is healthy and what is not.

✓ Actively (by speaking and/or writing) refute every idea that does not represent a healthy sense of identity for you, and you may have to keep doing this regularly for some time to get yourself to the place where you want to be.

✓ Identify pictures, words or phrases that represent what you deem to be your best sense of identity. Put these resources in conspicuous spaces around you so you see them often, because our exposures influence our beliefs. Then create a system for interacting with them regularly by reading, confessing, or a combination of the ways that work best for you to consistently keep them in mind.

✓ Identify external resources e.g., people in your life, books, podcasts, messages that can be a source of fuel to help you see yourself as you desire to, or that represent a healthier sense of identity for you. Schedule opportunities to regularly interact with these resources. For people, this could happen through phone calls, lunch meetups, reading or listening to their resources.

✓ Watch yourself; and every time you catch yourself repeating any unhealthy description of yourself whether aloud or in your mind, stop and counteract it with the new description you have identified. Do the same when you hear others say negative things about you – especially those who are authority figures over you. Even if you cannot counteract them to their faces for whatever reasons, counteract the effect of their words by refusing to take them in, instead repeat to yourself your new statement of identity. Below is a sample statement from one of my identity confessions that can guide you as you seek to create yours:

> *"I am loved, I am enough. I am able, I am enabled. I am strong, I am worthy, I am deserving of good things. I can do great things; I can be anything I want to be. I'm the best of my kind in the whole world."*

I encourage you to take time to build this foundation as you evolve into adulthood. It will help you to live above the clime and remain firm in the face of changing terrains. Do not let anything or anyone take away your positive sense of who you are and how you got here.

Find your identity by looking from within and reasoning with what is true about yourself. Also, harness the power of vision and confessions to continuously build a positive identity. Hold on to what you see and refuse to let anything take it from you. Know how to refuel when life happens, and when you feel your sense of identity shifting. You can achieve this through regular retreats with yourself, with friends, and/or wisdom from a trusted source.

> *Your identity is one of the key elements that will help you rock the decade of your twenties and the years that come after, so prioritise the fight for it beginning today!*

"But you are a chosen generation, a royal priesthood, a holy nation, His own special people..."
1 PETER 2:9 NKJV

Personal Reflection Questions

1. *What adjectives come to mind when you describe yourself?*

2. *Do these descriptions align with a healthy identity?*

3. *What new words can you use to describe yourself based on your learning from this chapter?*

4. *What one thing can you start doing today to fuel a healthier sense of self?*

Purpose

WHY AM I HERE?

PURPOSE IS THE BIG '*WHY*' BEHIND EVERYTHING we do. It is the intention or objective behind an action – or in this case, an existence. Although folks in previous generations may have had this question on their minds, I think that this generation has even more people who are discontent with living regular lives without connecting to a bigger WHY.

The convenience of technology has, possibly, freed up the human mind to think beyond the most basic needs, making our souls more awake to eternity than ever before. Whatever the drive, it is noble to lean in and explore this hunger for purpose because it has the potential to steer our lives in the direction of highest value.

When purpose is found and expressed, it manifests as a unique contribution to the world that has the potential to transcend a person's lifetime. For example, in Scriptures, Jesus defined His purpose as having come "to give life in abundance".[2] For Him, this was a driving centre for His work and investments. Paul also declared that he was called and chosen by God, "to preach the good news about Jesus to the Gentiles".[3] He centred his life around this assignment, eventually living and dying for it. Martin Luther King Jr. was another person who identified his purpose early in life and summed it up in his famous speech "I have a Dream".[4]

All three examples have had their contributions outlive them with their expressions impacting generations after them.

Purpose can be a compelling drive for our lives. It is what we find that makes life worth living and what we would die for if need be.

> *Every individual who consciously lives in the pursuit of purpose*

---

[2] *John 10:10*
[3] *Galatians 1:16*
[4] *Wikipedia.org | Martin Luther King Jr.*

> *positions themselves to respond to the call of a life that counts for more.*

However, many people are not as clear about their purpose from the onset like Jesus, Paul, or Martin Luther King Jr. Not being clear at the onset should not be considered as a deterrent because there are always opportunities to grow in the understanding of purpose.

Why Purpose?

Purpose gives each of us the opportunity to harness our uniqueness for the good of others. A journey of purpose is a means of communicating the recognition of our identity and the intentionality behind our creation to a world that desperately needs our individual contributions.

A person who seeks to live out their purpose is really saying, "I realise that I am not an accident, I am one significant of 8 billion, and I want to shine my light and spread my unique fragrance as the best use of the life I've been given, for the betterment of others." This shows that living purposefully is strongly connected to a healthy sense of identity.

God's purpose is to accomplish great things through each of us. He desires to use each life as evidence of His grace and expression of His love to all people. This expression gets more specific for each person, and though it is up to each of us to unravel the exact details of ours, we know that whatever we discover would be situated within this context of God's love and grace.

Therefore, while we seek to clarify and define our individual purposes, we can start contributing to our world by pursuing the general purpose that has been made clear to us on many fronts. The following scriptures give us clear guidance about God's intent:

- *"We are God's workmanship – created to do good works."* (Ephesians 2:10)

- *"If you are faithful in little things, you will be faithful in large ones. But if you are dishonest in little things, you won't be honest with greater responsibilities."* (Luke 16:10)

- *"Share each other's burdens, and in this way obey the law of Christ."* (Galatians 6:2)

From a careful consideration of the above verses, we can understand a few things about purpose even without knowing specific individualised details. First, we know that whatever a person's purpose may be, God's design is that it brings value to our world and the people in it. This is the starting point for anyone who desires to live out purpose – seek to do good and add value.

So, let me ask you – what are you doing today that makes life better for anyone at all, even if just one person on the earth? That, my friend, is you already taking baby steps in the right direction. If you cannot think of any, I'll encourage you to look for something to start with at this point in your life. It does not have to be big; it only needs to be a starting point.

Next thing to consider is – how well are you handling the things that you are currently working on? Depending on what stage of life you are in, this may be schoolwork, secular work, church work, or even housework. Because God's design is to give responsibility incrementally, whatever you have in your hands right now matters a lot.

How you handle today's little will determine how much more you can receive from God.

Finally, how well do you love people? To be honest, purpose cannot be centred around yourself. The very idea of purpose speaks to something that reaches beyond you - to the impact that you are making in the world. How can you receive something for a cause or people you do not care about?

Think about a time when you encountered someone who was functioning in a role and clearly did not care about the people they were responsible for. Maybe a teacher, caregiver or political leader? What did that look like? I am certain that they were unlikely to have left a positive impact on their constituency. Hence, the call of purpose needs you to identify a cause or people beyond yourself and your interests, that you deeply care about. Love for others prepares you to fully invest yourself in something that benefits them.

How Do We Find Purpose?

Purpose unfolds. While some people appear to have a full grasp about their purpose at an early stage, the specific dimensions unfold over time for most. However, this unfolding becomes clearer for those who intentionally put their hands to work.

Activating the unfolding of individual purpose often requires soul searching and personal reflection. For some, this may be an uneasy process because many times we are used to looking outward to find answers. Also, others may find this difficult because self-reflection typically takes patience and perseverance to get beneath the surface. However,

> *"The area of purpose is one where the answer is more likely to be within than without."*

Plus, self-reflection is an important life skill, so this is a good place to start practising. As you reflect, ask yourself the following questions and take notes:

1. **What attracts me?** What do you find yourself attracted to as you go about your regular day? What types of news items do you open as you scroll through notifications? What types of posts do you react to as you scroll on social media? What kind of people do you feel drawn to, or even jealous of – not because of their material possessions, but because of the work they are doing? Which topics do you struggle with remaining quiet about?

2. **What annoys me?** Is there an issue that consistently annoys you? Or a problem that causes you pain even when it is not personal to you? What do you regularly find yourself complaining about? What do you find yourself fighting against – even when your supposed opponent is not in the room?

3. **What awakens or energises me?** What can you work on for hours without realising the passage of time? Is there a task that is difficult for others or even despicable to them that comes easy to you? What would you freely contribute to without thinking of the cost even though it does cost you? What do you do that leaves you feeling refreshed even though you expend energy at it?

As a personal example, I stumbled on my purpose regarding building confident and resilient children accidentally, when I got the opportunity to teach weekly *Bible Clubs*[5] beginning from my late teenage years. I taught different groups of young children in mostly suburban settings and often had to deal with

---

[5] *Bible clubs are house-based gatherings where children learn about the Bible on a weekly basis.*

disrespectful behaviour. On many occasions, I had a huge lump in my chest as I made my way to meet these children. This was because I felt incapable of managing their behaviour and getting them to quietly listen through the duration of the lesson. However, I realised that no matter how each session went – and a good number of them did not go perfectly – I found myself exhausted in body, but excited at heart on the way home.

For all my trepidation and exhaustion, it never once crossed my mind to give up on any of the kids or not show up to teach them the next week. This realisation marked the beginning of my purpose discovery journey.

Now, your turn. Take some time to create an inventory of your attractions, annoyances, and awakeners. Do this over a definite period and continually pay attention as you learn more about yourself.

Once you find something that breaks your heart or sparks life in you, challenge yourself to invest some time in it against all odds. Options for investment include internship programs, volunteer opportunities, short courses, dedicated study, full time roles, etc. Whatever you do, try to incorporate a plan for investing in at least one thing that sparks your soul or heals your breaking heart in every season of your life. This will help to unveil your purpose in a quicker way and enable you to pay attention early to living for more.

As you begin to gain clarity around your purpose, it is important that you continue working at it on a consistent basis. Simply put, purpose is lived by keeping at it. Keep searching and finding and living, and in the process, you will be leaving your footprint on the sands of time. Be flexible, but also be committed. Learn not to leave things hanging, but to follow them to a reasonable conclusion. Train yourself to exercise staying power and to galvanise resources in the direction of a valuable cause, but also learn to recognize when it is time to move on.

Purpose Partners

Although your journey through fulfilling purpose is personal, it does not have to be lonely. From biblical history, we see that even Moses had his Aaron; Joshua had a Caleb; and Jesus had Peter, James, and John. Having people to walk with, lean on, and draw support from, is always a good thing. These people can spur you on when you are tired and remind you of why you first began.

Intentionally choose these relationships and invest in them systematically so that you can get the best out of them. In addition, take time to share your dreams in these contexts and ask for feedback as you take steps in the direction of purpose. Sharing helps you to better articulate what you are pursuing and gives you an opportunity to create a system of accountability around your pursuit; while feedback helps you to evolve faster and avoid unnecessary pitfalls.

"For we are Gods masterpiece. He has created us anew in Christ Jesus, so we can do the good things He planned for us long ago"
EPHESIANS 2:10

Personal Reflection Questions

1. *What am I doing today that benefits others, without directly benefiting me?*

2. *Which one issue in the world really breaks my heart or makes me smile, even when I'm not directly connected to it?*

3. *Which deliberate investment can I contribute to this issue on a regular basis, starting today?*

4. *Who in my life can I share my decision with, and can provide me with accountability and encouragement as I begin my purpose journey?*

Career

WHAT ABOUT WORK?

WHEN I WAS A CHILD, THE ANSWER TO "What do you want to be when you grow up?" seemed like a multiple-choice question with standard options – doctor, lawyer, engineer, teacher, etc. Today, the same question feels more theoretical with unlimited response options. While this development is good, it can put extreme pressure on young adults because choosing a career path now feels like being forced to pick a single dish at a lavishly catered buffet. This is still advantageous because it reinforces the truth that there is really no limitation as to what one can be, and there is not just one thing that a person should be.

To take advantage of these times is to fully explore your potential and current possibilities. Avoid the trap of being limited by societally prescribed options when you can be more. In addition, know that the definition of *work* has changed, especially with the advent of remote work, a global economy, the knowledge movement, and continuously evolving reward systems. These evolving realities should influence how career decisions are made.

No matter what stage you are – whether you are still considering which career path to take, or you are stepping into the "real world" with a degree that you may or may not be excited to work with – I invite you to consider the idea that…

> *"…a career is what you build while contributing your skills and abilities to solve real problems that real people are facing in the world."*

Think about it – musicians exist because entertainment meets a need in the lives of many people, pilots exist because people need to travel faster, and teachers exist because a good amount of people want education. When you think this way, you realise that your career path does not have to be static, because human needs are dynamic. You do not need to be overwhelmed about where you venture into the workforce from, as there will always be opportunities for growth and development. Instead of focusing on the title you would like to bear, or the reputable company you would give almost anything to work with, it is better to determine where and how you would like to contribute your unique giftings and skills to make the world a better place. This paradigm will set you up for success as you begin to consider what major (course) to study at the University (if you start asking this early), which classes to take while in the University, what work/volunteer opportunities to explore or turn down, what kind of jobs to pursue, or when to change roles.

More so, career is a societal construct that you can refine to fit your purposes. Imagine you were given one-fifth of a week to commit to building something with your name on it consistently while being paid for it. If you are like most people with a 40-hour work week, the time you spend at work constitutes approximately 24% of your entire week. You can extrapolate this and consider yourself spending

~24% of your most productive years at work. With the mindset that your work is your contribution to the world, plus an attitude that reflects this understanding, you can challenge yourself to create a legacy with what others may consider as the boring routine of work.

While considering what legacy to build, it may be important for you to take off the pressure about what 'legacy' looks like. Leaning on the words of Martin Luther King Jr., I would like to illustrate a perspective of legacy that is certainly noble, although unpopular. He said, "If a man is called to be a street sweeper, he should sweep streets even as Michelangelo painted, or Beethoven composed music or Shakespeare wrote poetry. He should sweep streets so well that all the hosts of heaven and earth will pause to say: 'Here lived a great street sweeper who did his job well'". This demonstrates that no single person has the monopoly of rights to legacy building, and in doing what we do well, we can all come close to legends such as Michelangelo and Shakespeare – not necessarily in the eyes of all men, but then, who knows? Even the Scriptures say…

"Do you see a man diligent in his work? He shall stand before kings and not mean men"
PROVERBS 22:29 NKJV

How then can we approach work with a legacy-building mindset?

Consider your work to be noble

Our minds are our greatest assets, and the stories we tell ourselves have the greatest power to define us. What you think about your work determines the energy you bring to it and the mastery you create with it. Therefore, to make anything great out of the work you do, you must first think of it as good and worthy of effort. So, what is it that you do? If it is legitimate, you are on the right track, and you must guard against anything that makes you feel ashamed of it. Even if it is not your best choice, you can consider it as a gift in this season and a tool that you can leverage to create value. More so, your work does not define you, rather, you define your work by the skill and excellence you apply to it.

Having clarified the above points, it is necessary to add that as you embrace your current reality, you should also be deliberate about figuring out exactly what you want and focusing on it. Be careful to ensure that complacency does not trap you in a place that ought to be temporary and a stepping stone. And then, be courageous in the pursuit of what you desire.

Bring your best to the job and master your craft

Work was given to man right after he was created. This shows that work is a crucial part of our existence, and it is something we all have a personal relationship with.

To prove this, think about the last time you had a holiday that lasted too long. Or the last time you were sick and unable to do anything for yourself. It might have felt good to have free time for the first few days, but how did it feel as the period stretched out? How did you feel on your first day back to work?

If work is something we are gifted with for our own sakes, then we have a responsibility to at least do well and get better at what we do.

No matter what you do, make sure you show up every day with your very best, and a commitment to get better at it.

Be prepared to take on more

I love this famous quote by Jonas Salk, *"The reward for work well done is the opportunity to do more."*

Scripture alludes to this when it says,

> *"For whoever has, to him more will be given, and he will have abundance; but whoever does not have, even what he has will be taken away from him"*
> **MATTHEW 13:12 NKJV**

If you are doing well with what you've been given and it results in your work multiplying, don't despair, increasing responsibility is a testimony to your competence, and evidence that your promotion is on its way. Be confident enough to ask for more work and seek out opportunities and roles in line with the legacy you intend to build.

As you do this, endeavour to craft your own narrative so you can effectively market yourself when the opportunity presents itself. As much as you work well, it is equally important that you tell your story and communicate the value that you bring to the table.

Be discerning while you work

According to Merriam Webster dictionary, to discern is *"to come to know or recognize mentally"*. The ability to see beyond what is obvious to the physical eye is a key element that every wise builder needs. As we go about our work, there will be relationships to foster or abandon, risks to take, skills to acquire, pits to avoid, opportunities best perceived and acted upon before they become obvious to all.

A person who acts by discernment is likely to set themselves apart from the rest by taking timely steps in favourable directions. In other words, it is not enough to show up at work every day and put in your best, you must be mentally and spiritually cognizant of the space in which you work to set yourself apart. Social awareness is an attribute of emotional intelligence that relates to *picking up emotional cues, understanding the needs of others and recognizing group dynamics.*[6] It is a valuable skill that can be learned.

Additionally, by reading relevant materials and staying current with evolving trends in a field, it is possible to understand, predict events and take targeted action ahead of time. However, there is a level of discernment that can only be gained by supernatural revelation. If you can acquire this in

---

[6] *HelpGuide.org | Improving Emotional Intelligence (EQ)*

addition to all else, it will be an added advantage for your career progress.

Understand that you are the constant in your career story, so prioritise your personal development

You are your greatest asset; hence, it is important to intentionally invest in your personal development and competence. Do not remain comfortable with ignorance, rather put yourself on the spot and push yourself to learn.

While it is okay not to know, it is not okay to remain ignorant. Be the person who says, "I don't know right now, but give me a few days and I'll find out." Remember that the most valuable thing you will walk away with from any job is yourself – not a salary earned, not an award nor a recognition. Embrace opportunities to improve your level of skill and expand your mental capacity as often as you can.

> *Do not put your personal growth on the back burner while chasing temporal relevance.*

Do not trade your soul

In the world of work, there will always be negotiations to be made and sometimes compromises too. This is okay, as long as you bear in mind what is negotiable for you and what is not. While you build, remember that nothing is worth the value of your soul. You should first sit with yourself and determine what constitutes your soul. What is your core, without which there would essentially be nothing left of you? For some, it is their personal value system, for others it is family, or a relationship with God, or a combination of these and more. Whatever it is, decide beforehand what you cannot give and keep it at the forefront of your mind. Weigh your opportunities, investments, and sacrifices against it. Know when to say no, and when to leave the table by deciding and affirming what is non-negotiable for you – first to yourself, and then to the world.

Ordinarily, we should expect that the reality of the changing work terrain would reflect in educational systems across the world since they are primarily directed at preparing individuals for work and problem-solving. However, this is not always the case, and many people are saddled with taking responsibility for their career readiness even though they are part of an educational system.

Thankfully, we live in an information age, so there is almost nothing that is inaccessible for one who is serious about learning. If you find yourself in this position, don't despair, rather invest in courses, books, mentorship, and begin to apply yourself as soon as you can. Volunteer, intern, try out a self-driven project, do whatever you can to make sure you start exercising your problem-solving muscles and contributing to the world even when there is no pressure on you to do so. By doing this, you will be preparing yourself to build the legacy you ultimately desire. I love the wisdom in the following phrases and would love to share them with you as motivation for you whenever you may feel stuck on your career journey:

- *Consistency trumps talent*
- *Innovation is key*
- *Value is irresistible*

Bearing these in mind will help you develop the right attitude and take actions that will positively influence your career in the long-term.

"Whatever you do, do well. For when you go to the grave, there will be no work or planning or knowledge or wisdom"

ECCLESIASTES 9:10

Personal Reflection Questions

1. *What is your current relationship with work?*

2. *What is the predominant attitude you bring to your education/work? How has it served you so far?*

3. *If your career trajectory is a legacy building exercise, what one thing could you do differently to incorporate this idea in practice?*

Relationships

DO I REALLY NEED FRIENDS?

IT IS OFTEN SAID THAT *"YOU ARE THE AVERAGE OF THE five people you spend the most time with."* Because we live in a world full of people, our day-to-day interactions occur in the context of relationships.

> Everywhere we go and in virtually everything we do; people are an indispensable part of our existence.

As a result, our ability to exist in peaceful relationships plays a significant role in the outcomes of our lives, and those who can derive real value from ordinary relationships often have an advantage. Apart from the people we encounter in our everyday lives and the effect that our ability to relate with them has on us, there is the added place of those we consistently allow to pour into our lives. These people have the greatest potential to make or break us especially in the long-term. We were often reminded of this as teens with the mantra, *"Your friends can make or mar you."*

Depending on your personality and experiences, you may or may not even gravitate towards friends. If you have ever had an experience that made you swear off friends for life, you are welcome to my party, lol.

At some point in my life, I came to the decision that I was never going to have a 'best friend' again. This was my takeaway from two consecutive years of having friends who stopped being my best friends because we had disagreements, or we inadvertently grew apart.

In my mind, the prior investment and subsequent pain when I lost those friendships was too costly, and I was never going to put myself in that situation again. However, years later when I found myself surrounded with several amazing people who were willing to be my friends, I ended up having to rework my mindset in a way that helped me enjoy my new relationships. On the other side of that process, I am so glad that I did not keep running away.

Now I know for sure that we need to be deliberate about relationships, because I have experienced time and again the blessings that can flow through them when we get them right.

Most of our relationships can be broadly categorised as:

✓ Upwards
✓ Sideways
✓ Downwards

These categorizations do not indicate the worth or intrinsic value of people, rather they demonstrate the predominant direction of value flow in relation to oneself.

For relationships in the upwards category, we are more likely to gain value from them – whether intellectual, financial, motivational, or any other type of value. Again, this does not mean that you do not contribute anything to these relationships, it is a simplistic categorization that attempts to describe what happens most of the time. In sideways relationships, the exchange of value tends to be more mutual between parties, while in downwards relationships, we are likely to give out more than we receive.

Keep in mind that these categories are not necessarily static, and it is possible for people to move between them with the passage of time. For example, you may typically relate with a younger sibling using a downward approach. However, as they grow older and the dynamics of your relationship transitions, a change in approach to "sideways" could be necessary. A mentor-mentee relationship may also evolve over time to become a mutual friendship.

> *Taking out the time to evaluate and categorise relationships in our lives is a significant step towards harnessing their potential.*

As you become an adult, it is very likely that the most significant relationships in your life will cease to be in your face. For example, you may no longer live with your immediate family, or attend the same classes with your best friend, you may even live in a different city from your most trusted mentor. This means that nurturing these relationships will require more intentional action on your part.

It is important to note here that there is great value in approaching any relationship with a wholesome self. In other words, it is more beneficial that you do not approach a human relationship with an expectation for anyone to fix you or give you hope in yourself.

Honestly, that role belongs to God and yourself, and putting that burden on other humans may be too much for them and disappointing to you. This point refers us back to Theme One and the necessity of developing a healthy sense of identity. Mastering your identity teaches you to be at peace with and in love with yourself and these traits translate to a radiating sense of wholeness. When you know and love yourself, you are better able to find the highest version of you and bring that person to your various relationships.

This is not meant to imply that you cannot be vulnerable with others; it just means that you are not seeking ultimate validation from them. By itself, a healthy sense of identity takes off undue pressure and gives your relationships space to breathe.

Another thing to note is that the best relationships involve two-sided exchange of value. Great relationships are built on give and take and should be as much as possible a win-win for both parties. Additionally, it is wise to intentionally seek out relationships in categories where you are deficient and to create definite plans and structures for investing in these significant relationships.

Having discussed the importance of relationships and how to approach them, I would like to expatiate on a few different kinds of relationships and how you can build them up.

1. Family members

Depending on the nature of the family you grew up, relationships with parents or siblings may or may not be a given. For some, you may have had older siblings who always took advantage of younger ones, for others, it may have been younger siblings who got stuff from everyone and gave nothing in return, because well, they had nothing to give. As you grow older, the onus lies on you to either begin to mine the gold resident in these relationships or to sit on a gold mine without having any idea.

You can begin the mining process by examining your current relationship with close family members to see where you are at. Also take a moment to step out of the *"see finish"*[7] context in which you probably relate with family members and view them through the lens of an outsider. What are their strengths? In what ways have they added value to you that you failed to recognize? What are the things they struggle with? What will your relationship look like in the next five years if things remain as they are now? Are you satisfied with what you see?

The answers to these questions will guide you on the next steps in building or rebuilding your relationship from this point. I strongly believe that family is God's first gift to help us learn the art of giving, receiving, caring and being cared for, and successfully practising these skills "at home" will very likely be of benefit in the context of other relationships. However, it is true that family contexts and early life experiences differ and for some, certain dynamics might not allow you to be best friends with family members. If that's the case, while you accept this reality, do all you can to

---

[7] *See finish – Nigerian pidgin for "overfamiliarity"*

not harbour resentment against them in your heart because that would be unhealthy and harmful to you in the long-term.

2. Professional colleagues

This group is important both for the sheer amount of time we spend with them, as well as their capacity to influence the progress of our work. Peers, superiors, and subordinates at work generally fall into this category. While discernment is needed in all relationships, it is extremely important in this case because a lack of it can be immediately costly. It is good to be civil in this context as in all others – wear a smile, be respectful, do not look down on others, do not talk badly of others, bring your best self, and truly care.

However, you must be wise enough to discern personalities and motives. Do not be overly suspicious but do well to apply caution and wisdom in how you present yourself. Also, understand and uphold your priorities in the right order. While it may happen that a co-worker or colleague becomes your best friend, do not start out hoping for people to particularly be all friendly with you. Respect professional relationships for what they are: an alliance to get the job done. Unless a time comes where you reassess and realise a need to review your priorities, make sure that your alliance does not detract from this aim. Also, if you realise that your priority has changed, figure out the next best step and act quickly so that you do not do a disservice to the organisation you are supposed to be serving.

3. Personal friends

These are likely your most important relationships at this stage. They are the ones you (should) choose for yourself because of their potential to push or pull you, to influence the direction of your thoughts and aspirations, to support you through the good and bad, and to remain constant through the changing seasons of life. It is important to know yourself in the context of these relationships and avoid putting pressure on yourself to be something that you are not.

While some people attract friends like honey does bees, others struggle with maintaining even one consistent friendship, and that's okay! For those who are like honey, knowing yourself involves recognizing that you naturally attract people. Based on this awareness, you can be deliberate about assessing those in your space and determining what level of access is wise to allow each person.

For those who are more inclined to be by themselves, knowing yourself involves paying attention to the people around you, and knowing when it is time to go the extra mile to initiate or sustain a closer relationship. *Intentionality* is the keyword. When you know what you desire, hold it in your awareness, and take practical steps in its direction, you are more poised to gain what you seek in terms of finding wholesome relationships than you would ever be by merely hoping for the best.

4. Mentors

A mentoring relationship is one that provides guidance and direction based on a mentor's wisdom and life experience. While some have described submitting to mentors for specific areas including career mentors, business mentors, spiritual mentors, marriage mentors, others have described having life mentors in more of a one-fits-all model. Mentorship could also be formal or informal, with informal mentorship involving a less direct ask or structure to the relationship. This could also involve remote interaction with a mentor's guidance communicated through books, podcasts, interviews, messages, etc.

While formal mentorship seems to be more glamorous, informal mentorship also holds great potential that many do not pay attention to. If the idea of mentorship is based on standing on the shoulders of those who have gone before, then we see that on a closer look, it is possible to have potential mentors in our space who may have been ignored or taken for granted because they did not look "grand". Informal mentorship also prepares us for formal mentoring relationships by helping us to understand how people think and to know what they prioritise.

To make the best of mentoring relationships, it is crucial to take responsibility for your personal growth and ensure you communicate that in your interactions. Don't expect your mentor to spoon-feed you or make everything convenient for you. Be respectful of the fact that they have other things going on in their lives outside their commitment to you and consider every moment you are given as a premium. Give due consideration to the ideas they share with you, provide feedback about your implementation, and give credit to them when you can do so.

Additionally, be on the lookout for ways to appreciate them. This could begin with small things like celebrating milestones, sending congratulatory messages, showing up at their events, giving feedback about something they have done, thank you cards and emails, etc. Remember, no relationship is sustainable in the long term when there is a one-directional flow of value.

5. Mentees

At this stage in life, you may first scowl at the idea of having mentees, and that is understandable. However, you should consider the idea that when you pour into another based on a prior experience you have navigated, you may be doing the work of a mentor and serving a mentee. While you do not need to fixate on the title, it is important to think about giving back as you go on your journey, even if this starts in the smallest of ways.

This is a good way to multiply the efforts of those who have helped you walk your path, and a significant way to show your gratitude. More so, it ensures that you live as a channel rather than a tank and creates more room for the guidance and investments you seek to find their way to you.

A simple idea is to commit to help anyone who is going through something you have experienced and succeeded at. Another is to think about who you wish you had in your life in a particular season and make a conscious decision to be that person to someone who is in the same shoes. You can start making this kind of investment at any level at all.

6. Random people

First things first – Be kind to everyone, you have no idea who today's stranger will become tomorrow. Might be your angel, your best friend or the one who presides over something that is important to you.

Even if they do not become anything to you, you may have unknowingly eased the burden of a co-sojourner in this territory and that in itself is worth your effort. Plato aptly instructs about this in his words,

> *"Be kind, for everyone you meet is fighting a battle you know nothing about."*

Also, take time to build trust – never feel so carried away that you share your entire life with a stranger because of what they appear to be. Realise that people you see every day may fall into the category of "stranger". If you have not had the chance to see proof of a person's character, it is wise to be careful about how much of yourself you allow them access.

Apart from the six highlighted above, I am sure there are other kinds of relationship contexts that are relevant. Feel free to add those to the list and think through how to make the best of them based on the principles discussed so far.

The following rules for relationship building provide guidance on navigating relationships in general:

✓ **Always, always, seek to add value:** Value addition can be in the form of sharing resources, helping with projects, giving gifts, extending compliments, providing a shoulder to lean on in difficult times, etc. Scripture admonishes that *"it is more blessed to give than to receive"*[8] and while we often think about this in terms of religious or charitable giving, giving in the context of our relationships also beautifully illustrates this truth. If you've ever had a chance to be a cheerleader that helped someone win during a

---

[8] *Acts 20:35*

tough time, I'm sure you can relate to the blessedness of being on this side. Ask yourself often, "how can I add value to this person?" This is a sure-fire way to become one who is blessed in and by relationships.

On an aside note, I know that many people don't know what to do when someone they love is going through a hard time, so they end up staying away because it is the simpler option. In my experience this is not the best way to add value, so I can tell you for certain–don't do it. You don't have to know what to say or do, but you should let the person you love see that you care enough to show up even when you have no words or clear direction. By doing so, you give them the opportunity to tell you how best to care for them while you remain at their side.

✓ **Know when to be vulnerable, and forgive in advance:** Relationship building unfortunately comes with vulnerability which is obviously risky, but as the old saying goes, *"nothing ventured, nothing gained"*. The most beautiful relationships are those where unguarded people share their weaknesses and strengths while covering for each other. Sharing vulnerability requires trust and creates a possibility for intended and unintended offence, thus necessitating a readiness to forgive from the outset. Because no human being is perfect, there is no assurance that your vulnerability, when shared, will never be trampled on or used against you. However, you must be able to assess each situation on its own merit and realise when there has been an honest mistake.

Furthermore, you must resist the temptation to recoil into your shell because your trust was once broken. After forgiving and letting go, be discerning and willing to try again with better application of wisdom if need be. Another benefit of vulnerability is that it positions you to receive from others and reap benefits from a relationship where you already invest.

✓ **Maintain boundaries:** I saw a definition of boundaries somewhere which goes thus, *"Boundaries are the distance at which I can love you and me simultaneously."*[9] They are an important part of building relationships because they help to preserve your soul as you seek to bond with another.

---

9 Prentis Hemphill

Boundaries will keep you from being vulnerable with an unproven person, and help you restrict access after a person has proven themselves to be unworthy of trust. Boundaries will help you give value without exhausting yourself and teach you when and where to draw the line. They will prevent you from losing yourself in the name of friendship and protect you from the pitfalls of naivety as you navigate new relationships. As they are an essential part of your relationship toolkit, do yourself a favour and learn to use them from now.

✓ **Do not lose yourself:** If you ever find that you are losing the essence of you in a relationship, that is very likely a good sign to take a break or move on. Do they constantly ignore your boundaries, do they take and never give, or do they drain the energy out of you? Are their ideals opposite of yours and there is no way to maintain your integrity in association with them? Part of being relationship-wise is knowing when it is time to move on. Also, know that moving on does not mean you have failed, it just means that you value yourself enough to do what is best for you even when it hurts.

- ✓ **Be patient and considerate:** Do not be in a hurry to build friendship! After all, good things typically take time to build, and a new acquaintance may not be as prepared as you are to go the entire mile at the beginning. As you seek to build relationships, be considerate of other people's time, personalities, prior experiences, and present circumstances so that you do not judge them to be unfriendly when it just happens that the time isn't right for them. Also be patient – different plants require varying time periods to blossom. Some relationships require a longer investment period than others before the parties involved can start reaping from them.

- ✓ **Be cognizant of seasons:** Know that some relationships come in seasons and be ready to let go when a season has changed. This does not mean that you easily give up on every relationship by determining that its time is over. Certain relationships are for life, and you should identify those and fight for them as much as possible. However, the dynamics of even *for-life* relationships can change over time, and it is important to be willing to adapt in order to sustain them. Always mind how you close a door; because you never know when you'll need to go through it again or help another to go through.

✓ **Not everyone will like you, and that is perfectly okay:** Never let your sense of worth be dependent on another person's perception of you. That way, when certain people do not like you or your relationships with them do not work out, you can take it in good faith and not allow someone else's response to define how you see yourself.

> "Two are better than one, because they have a good return for their labour.... If either of them falls down, one can help the other up. But pity anyone who falls and has no one to help them up"
> **ECCLESIASTES 4:9**

Personal Reflection Questions

1. *Who are the five people you spend the most time with on average?*

2. *In what ways do you add value to them and vice versa?*

3. *Based on the future you see for yourself, what would you do differently to strengthen the impact or minimise the influence that these relationships have on you?*

4. *Is there someone currently outside your immediate circle that would be a significant contribution to the future you desire? How can you start investing in a relationship with them today?*

Love

FOREVER AND ALWAYS?

IN SECONDARY SCHOOL, 'PAIRING' WAS A TERM WE used to describe hanging out exclusively with a guy or girl. It was one of those concepts that looked different to adults and students. On the part of our parents and teachers, pairing was completely bad, but to us as students, it was a fun and often reputable idea.

Having passed through that phase to arrive at the point where it becomes normal and even expected to be in a 'significant other' relationship, there could be a sense of dissonance. We can move beyond the dissonance by realising that in this season of life, it is completely natural to develop a genuine desire to find the one person we can share life with, for life. This desire is great, as it is often a necessary drive to actively seek out a life partner. However, it is important that it also drives us to act wisely and position ourselves to derive the highest level of value from this special relationship.

To begin with, let us examine general reasons for marriage which is the ideal endpoint of an exclusive relationship. Marriage is good for companionship, for sexual expression and procreation. The following Scriptures speak to this:

> "It is not good for the man to be alone. I will make a helper who is just right for him."
> **GENESIS 2:18**

> "But if a man thinks that he's treating his fiancée improperly and will inevitably give in to his passion, let him marry her as he wishes."
> **1 CORINTHIANS 7:36**

> "And God blessed them, and God said unto them, "Be fruitful, and multiply, and replenish the earth."
> **GENESIS 1:28**

A close look at the above contexts makes it clear that marriage is not primarily intended to complete an individual, nor was it designed to provide for their material needs or satisfy societal expectations about what people should do with their lives.

Truthfully, there is no one in this world who can essentially complete another person, including a spouse. The fairy-tale idea of a princess waiting for a prince to save her from an unfortunate circumstance and lead her into 'happily ever after' is simply fairy-tale. In real life, marriage is a mutual commitment to give and take for the benefit of each other. In addition, it is a melting pot of the strengths and flaws of the involved parties, and an opportunity to build alongside a chosen companion.

So, while a spouse can love, care for, and add immense value to you, they can never fill the place in you that constitutes your essence. Only you—*and God*—can do that. This means that your spouse cannot be your ultimate source of validation and self-worth. While it is ideal for them to complement you, it is more important for you to develop yourself such that if for any reason they do not, you would still feel confident and secure in yourself. Since what you come into a relationship with largely determines what you get out of it, know that an investment in yourself is an investment in your love relationship as well.

Another worthwhile truth is this: regardless of what society says, marriage is not a compulsory course in the university of life. If you prefer not to pursue this kind of relationship in a season or for life, it does not mean that there is something wrong with you.

Also, if you desire it but it is not happening as you imagined it would, there is nothing wrong with you either. Do not put unnecessary pressure on yourself to find love for the sake of finding love. In the words of a favourite author, *"Thou shalt marry is **not** the eleventh commandment."*[10]

You can focus on living your life to its fullest and making the best use of this gift of time and life while seeking to attain your desire for marriage. Be careful to recognize and mitigate the temptations that you are susceptible to in a season when it feels like love is not finding you by first acknowledging how you feel. Then, avoid the trap of leaning into any available person when you clearly know that they are not right for you. Instead, guard your heart and resist the lure

---

[10] *Olajumoke Adenowo | Beyond My Dreams.*

of emotional entanglement in the absence of commitment. And of course, don't commit to a person who is not worthy of you. I know from personal experience that this may not be easy because I had to practice it one time when I met someone who appeared to be a great fit but showed signs that were not consistent with who they claimed to be. After walking away with my head high, I got home and cried my eyes out. As painful as it was at the time, I'm forever glad that I made the right decision.

> **Do not commit to a person who is not worthy of you.**

For those who are interested, the journey from *single* to *married* is always a process. Often, people go through one or more exploratory relationships before making a marriage commitment. Whatever this is called in your context (e.g., seeing, dating, friendship, 'relationship', courting, etc.), navigating with wisdom is important to prevent compromise while allowing for a healthy exploration. This time can be deliberately leveraged to enable you make an informed decision about a potential partner using the following guidelines:

✓ **Love yourself:** Actually, this applies across the board, whether you are seeking a marriage relationship or not. To love yourself is to acknowledge that you are worthy of love, and to treat yourself like you would any other person you love. It involves being aware of your strengths and flaws and accepting them while refusing to sell yourself short or settle for someone who does not recognize you as valuable. It also involves choosing to do what is best for you even when your emotions or any external factors tempt you to do otherwise.

✓ **Build friendship first:** Make deliberate attempts to *learn* a person you are considering a relationship with, just like you know your other friends. Ask questions. Communicate, communicate, communicate! Do not let the potential and possibility of what is ahead prevent you from gaining a clear-headed perspective of the present.

✓ **Trust the process:** Understand that growth takes time, so do not be in a hurry. Be careful about meeting someone today and deciding tomorrow that they are the one for you. Allow a relationship to develop naturally, deliberately invest in getting to know the other person, pay attention to the clues they give you, and give yourself the opportunity to see them when they are not at their best.

✓ **Know your worth:** You are a well-thought-out creature of an intentional God, and you are extremely loved. Do not ever give yourself to someone just because you desire validation or acceptance. In the same vein, don't let anyone's rejection break you. Instead, feel bad for them because they missed out on someone amazing! You are by yourself loved and complete; ruminate on this knowledge and let it liberate you.

✓ **Set boundaries and be confident about communicating and enforcing them:** For your own good, there are levels of intimacy that are better reserved for marriage. Determine beforehand what these are and maintain boundaries that help you stay away from them. Also know that emotional intimacy can fuel physical intimacy, so beware of letting your emotions run wild when you are not yet fully committed to someone. Don't go an inch if you do not intend to go a mile.

✓ **Recognize that while the responsibility for your final choice lies with you, wisdom is profitable to direct**. Listen to those around you, especially those who have known and loved you before this person came along, to help you judge their character and sincerity of heart.

✓ **Understand that this one relationship is not enough to provide you with all the support that relationships can provide**. Be intentional about your other meaningful relationships and don't let them die out while you build this one.

It is often said that *"When a person shows you who they are, believe them the first time."* I would modify that to say,

> **"...pay attention to what they show you, and don't lie to yourself."**

While trying to decipher a person's character, it is wise to not take certain words or actions for granted, and to probe further when you are uncomfortable with what you see. Maybe ask someone that knows them better, or ask people that know you better, or talk to them to see what underlies their behaviour.

Whatever you do, listen to your inner witness, and do not take a step further when there is evidence of character flaws that unsettle you. Many young people have ended up in unwholesome relationships that have been detrimental to their destinies by ignoring this rule.

Start creating a list early in life about what matters the most to you – even before you actively start pursuing a love relationship. As you grow, the list may change, and that is fine; it just tells you more about yourself and how you are maturing.

Also, it would be wise for most traits on your list to be weightier than just physical attributes. Look out for these traits as you begin to interact with whoever you are considering an exclusive relationship with. What does the person consistently show? If possible, make efforts to observe them in a variety of environments. Do not be blinded by their behaviour only when they are with you, instead try to observe them with their family, friends, co-workers, in traffic, and even with support staff. How they behave with these other people can let you know who they truly are.

If you have good reason from your observations to believe that they have traits that you cannot live with, make sure to seek counsel, and be prepared to take your leave if necessary. Many who go ahead into marriage despite signs that their partners have significant negative traits end up suffering in silence or walking right back out when they can't deal anymore. Don't let this be you.

Another thing your list helps you realise is the person you ought to become while you wait to find love. Because we are so different, it's hard to give a prescription about what traits we should develop to best serve our future spouses. However, I believe there are a few universal characteristics that would make anyone a better person and partner. Like:

Kindness

My simple definition of kindness is: *"consistently treating others well"*. We all want to be treated well, but it takes a kind person to be able to serve others what they wish for themselves, and this truly makes the difference in everyday life. Remember, people are often fighting battles that no one knows, so practising kindness should be a way of life.

> *Kindness is "consistently treating others well".*

[11]

Respect

To respect a person is to *duly regard their feelings, wishes or rights.*[11] Being respectful to others has nothing to do with their status or age, it is a conscious decision to see them as valuable and reflect that in interactions with them.

A respectful person will not treat you as less because of differences in opinions, personalities, preferences, or whatever else you disagree on.

Responsibility

It takes a mature person to be willing and able to take responsibility for their words, thoughts, and actions. Honestly, it is stressful to be in a relationship with someone who blames every and any event on external forces; because they will never feel enabled to effect change from within.

A person who can take responsibility for their errors is more likely to *apologise* and *course-correct* compared to one who never sees themselves as being at fault.

---

[11] *Oxford Languages via Google.*

No one really wants to live with someone who cannot change directions when there is need.

Conversely, a person who is constantly disrespectful, self-centred and refuses to take responsibility should warrant careful consideration, conversation, counsel and visible change before commitment happens – except you are sure that you are completely fine with living with these characteristics, which is very unlikely.

Finally, take your time to make the right decision about the person you marry. Yes, marriage is a beautiful thing, and two are better than one; however, this beauty only shines forth when it is cultivated right.

Take wise steps in the direction of finding a spouse by showing up, developing yourself to become a better person who adds value to others, investing in your current relationships, etc., but do not become desperate, as desperation is likely to blindside you and lead you into a ditch. Love yourself, follow due process, and let love happen for you.

Do not settle for less because that would be a short-term solution to a long-term situation.

Choose to live fully and enjoy life no matter what side of the love aisle you are on. This choice will make your life count for more.

"Marriage should be honoured by all and the marriage bed kept undefiled..."
HEBREWS 13:4 NKJV

Personal Reflection Questions

1. *On a scale of 1 to 10, how in love with yourself are you?*

2. *What traits are most important to you in a life partner?*

3. *To what level do you see yourself demonstrating the above traits?*

4. *Is there someone in your life who can give you an honest assessment when you're considering a relationship? How would you react to their assessment?*

Finance

MONEY MATTERS!

WHEN I WAS ABOUT 15 YEARS OLD, I stumbled upon "THE RICHEST MAN IN BABYLON" by George Samuel Clason. This was the first time it occurred to me that there were principles that governed wealth creation which I could start applying at my level.

A few months afterwards, I remember having to temporarily foot my own bills for a week and I was glad to have had enough funds to rely on because I had been practising what I learned. Although the years ahead showed me that there was much more to learn, this foundation gave me an advantage that I will always appreciate.

I'm sure you can also relate to the fact that nothing teaches you how much you do *not* know about finances as much as taking responsibility for your own expenses. Prior to this time, you may have known that money does not grow on trees, but the shift in responsibility makes that lesson clear on a whole new level. Although experiential learning is an acceptable way to gain knowledge, certain lessons are better learned from other people's experiences and expertise. Learning about finance early will set you up for financial freedom and help you gain time.

A good starting point for this discourse about finances is that "you are not how much you have". In other words, money does not define your identity. Think about what this means and come to terms with it early so that you can assign money to its appropriate place in your life.

Another important point is that money is a tool or vehicle that takes on the character of the person who owns it. Money is neither good nor bad, but it can become either depending on you. Therefore, who you are and how you organise your life are the building blocks of your journey to wealth creation.

They determine the value that money adds to you and the world around you.

Now to the basics – What is money, really? And why is it so relevant? How is it different from wealth?

Money can simply be defined as a unit of exchange for value. Everyone needs money to exchange for the value they desire, whether tangible e.g., clothes, food, personal items, or intangible e.g., services, knowledge, access. Wealth, however, is less rigid in definition because it is dependent on individual perspectives. While wealth can be universally defined as an abundance of valuable possessions or money, there is no standard criteria to qualify abundance.

Accordingly, to some, wealth is *having enough material resources to acquire whatever they want at any point in time.* To others, it is *the possession of resources in sufficient amounts as to be able to give consistently to those in need.* Yet, others see wealth as *an increasing flow of value that can be used to purchase influence and power.*

Feel free to fill in the blank and define what wealth means to you so that it can help you determine your direction as you figure out money matters. My preferred definition is…

> *"Wealth is 'access to all the resources that I need to carry out my God-given assignment'."*

This helps to maintain a balance between accumulation (which could be endless) and outflow (which should be continuous). It also brings up the important concept of contentment. Think about this – what defines the vastness of a person's wealth?

The richest man in the world today is so because his net worth is the highest in the known world. However, there is always the possibility that one of the 2 or 3 that are right behind him acquire more assets and take over the title – and this happens all the time. There is always more money to be desired and acquired, and those who live by the drive to get more will never find satisfaction with what they have, no matter how much it is. Consequently, the pursuit of wealth from a place of discontent is a sure recipe for an unhappy life because the target will keep moving, and there will never be a finish line in sight.

Having settled this foundation, we can now focus on responsible management of finances as a means of wisely stewarding the resources we have to make our lives more comfortable. Wealth is rarely ever an accidental production, so it is never too early to think about how to build it. More so, this phase of life is the best time to develop the thinking and habits that will set you up for a wealthy experience as you grow older.

The most basic source of financial inflow is income. However, creating wealth from income is not automatic. As a matter of fact, financial inflow is not necessarily a measure of wealth, as is how much is retained and/or converted into assets. For example, a person who earns $1,000 monthly but spends $800 monthly, is not as wealthy in monetary terms as one who earns $800 monthly and spends $500 monthly. How much is left is what makes the difference in the net worth of these two people, and this is not always directly proportional to how much they earn. To take it further, if any of these individuals invest some of their earnings in a venture that yields interest, they end up increasing their net worth, without necessarily increasing their income or minimising their expense.

4-Point Agenda

Applying wisdom to managing financial resources is not always complex. In fact, this 4-point agenda is a simple and quick guide to get you started no matter where you are: First, *Monitor*, then *Save*, then *Invest* and *Spend*!

✓ ***By Monitor***, I mean keep tabs on your finances. Know what comes in and what goes out. If you can, create a log, just to make sure you are familiar with your income and expenses no matter what level you are at. Also, decide beforehand what your spending limits should be and think twice before overshooting.

Do not make impromptu spending decisions under pressure, rather take time to ascertain if they align with your overarching values and goals. Spending to impress is always a no-no because it will almost surely lead to an unsustainable lifestyle. Depending on what you prioritise, it may also be important to create space for giving in your spending. Giving is a way of using your finances to create impact, influence, and leverage. A person whose wealth only serves to improve their own life is an example of one who is living for themselves alone; this is not the best way to set yourself up for a life of significance.

✓ *By Save,* I mean consistently set aside a portion of your financial inflow. Do not just have an aspiration but have a goal. You can start out with saving basically to increase your net worth, and you can divide it up into categories with time e.g., saving for a particular expense, for an emergency fund, for business capital, for investment opportunities, etc. Fund your savings before you begin your spending. It is perfectly okay to start small but aim for consistency and growth.

Be honest with yourself as you seek to save and ensure you are meeting up with set goals. This will take discipline, so if you are not sure that you have what it takes to maintain that discipline, create boundaries that assist you to do so.

Examples of boundaries include opening an account without a card, putting a spending limit on your account, instituting a standing order to deduct a percentage of your income into a savings account with restricted access, etc.

✓ ***By Invest,*** I mean find ways to make your money work for you. However, you need to ensure that whatever means you choose is legitimate and proven. Investments can be high or low risk, and those with higher risk often have higher returns. You should figure out your investor personality to determine what works best for you.

When you start out, it is useful to seek counsel from experienced friends, mentors, or professionals in the investment sector to help you make informed decisions about the best options. However, the final responsibility for your investment decisions lies with you, so make sure to do careful research and introspection before following any recommendation you receive.

✓ ***Finally, Spend!*** This needs no explanation. Money is meant to serve you, and God gives us richly all things to enjoy, so you should feel happy about using your finances to provide for yourself and those that are important to you.

Know that success is often a result of systems, and systems are created by boundary lines. As you build your life system, think about the following guidelines to position yourself for financial success:

1. Learn the virtue of contentment.

Contentment is the ability to be satisfied with one's possessions, status, or situation. Although it sounds like complacency, they are not the same. While complacency is an uninformed self-satisfaction, contentment is more informed and thus, takes steps towards a desired goal while maintaining a state of inner peace. Clearly, this is not a lesson that happens all at once, and that is okay. What is important is that you commit to learning contentment every time the opportunity presents itself.

Think about your motives when contemplating spending and earning opportunities. As you make financial decisions and take actions in the direction of your financial future, consistently check to ensure that greed or pride is not your driving force so that you don't end up somewhere you never intended to go.

2. Have a financial plan/goal.

What do you really want from your finances? Are you okay with having what you need to get through the day, week, or month? How much is sufficient for you? Are you someone that wants to have backup funds stashed away for the long term? Do you have financial obligations to certain people, e.g., family members or loan repayments? Do you want to consistently make charitable donations? Make notes about these and let them reflect in your financial plan.

3. Seek to create multiple value flows that can return diverse income streams.

While it is okay to start out with a single source of income, it is important to consider diversifying one's income streams with the passage of time. This helps to maximise revenue potential. As you venture into adulthood, consider learning a skill here or there, grooming a skill you already have, or pursuing a passion different from your steady path to contribute additional value that can be rewarded. Always look out for opportunities to create passive income.

4. Do not make an idol out of money.

At the risk of sounding cliché, I dare say that money is not everything. Do not start out seeking to get rich, rather seek to create and deliver value. Because money is a terrible slave master, those who are driven by it are likely to make poor choices that haunt them in the long term.

> *To be able to retain control of your life, you need to master money rather than have it master you, and this is easier to achieve if you do not make an idol out of it.*

"Beforehand, he called ten of his servants and gave them ten minas. 'Conduct business with this until I return,' he said"

LUKE 19:13

Personal Reflection Questions

1. *To what extent do your finances currently influence your view of yourself?*

2. *What is your best definition of wealth?*

3. *If you were to create a financial goal for 5 years from now, what would it look like? Write this out.*

4. *What can you start doing today in terms of saving, investing, gaining an additional skill set, or creating an additional income stream to get started on your goal?*

Faith

WHAT SHOULD I BELIEVE?

FAITH CAN BE DEFINED AS *COMPLETE TRUST OR confidence in someone or something.*[12] It is also a term that is commonly used to describe subscription and adherence to the core doctrines of a religion. Related to this, some people describe themselves as being "people of faith".

Practically, what does this mean?

> *The concept of faith is founded on belief in a greater force or power behind the creation and sustenance of the universe.*

---

[12] *Dictionary.com*

When you pause to observe nature and consider how the world works – the sun rotating on its axis, the earth revolving around the sun, the constant change in seasons, and the miracle of new life – it makes sense to conclude that there is a Superior Being responsible for the cycle of events that keep the universe in existence, and that Superior Being is God!

If this is true, then the next line of thought becomes "How do we relate to this Super Person?" This is the foundation of a conversation about faith. Faith in this sense refers to figuring and forging a relationship with the God, whom we do not see, but whose works we see.

Hence, a person of faith is one who actively pursues a relationship with the Creator and permits this relationship to influence their everyday life. In its fullest form, this becomes an anchor for the soul, and a lighthouse for the journey through this side of eternity. Let me explain this:

An *anchor* is a reliable or principal support; a fixed point that serves to hold an object firmly.[13] Because

---

[13] *Merriam Webster Dictionary*

we live in a changing world, we often experience desired and undesired changes, times when we feel out of control, situations that are unexpected, or just the wear and tear of growth and moving expectations.

With these, there is need for a point of reference, a constant that we can hold on to, a place or person we can approach with certainty regardless of the uncertainties that life brings.

Similarly, a *lighthouse* is a structure that gives a powerful signal which helps with navigation especially for sailors.[14] When a person journeys through the unknown – which life often is – a lighthouse is an asset because it ensures that they do not lose their way.

This is how faith serves as a source of strength and guidance through our journey on earth. Suffice to say – the fact that a sailor is lost at sea, or a weary traveller does not know the path through the desert does not negate the truth that there is a way out or a right path.

Likewise, when life's paths are unknown to us, it does not mean that they are not known to anyone

---

[14] *Merriam Webster Dictionary*

else. Thus, we circle back to our need for the Creator because surely, the One who made us should know. Deliberately engaging faith helps us to align our values and life pursuits with the heart of this One.

I acknowledge that some people see faith as a limiting and constraining concept that prevents them from enjoying all that life has to offer. This outlook may have resulted from faulty interactions with faith or people of faith that left them scarred and it is totally understandable.

However, this is an invitation to step out of that box for a bit and see the merits of a journey of faith (aka relationship with God). I am making this case because I know that its virtues are universal and counterfeit experiences should not deter anyone from seeking out this source of indescribable value.

As a Christian, the basis for my faith is an understanding that God has been seeking a relationship with man from the beginning of time. This is why He sent His Son, Jesus, to bridge the gap for us to become His children. For many Christians like me, and indeed people of other religious traditions, the principles of their chosen faith typically serve as a moral compass. But the truth is that there are tons of people who do not believe in God, or claim not to believe in anything at all, who act in the most excellent of ways. This highlights the fact that a practice of faith goes beyond external actions.

Additionally, I know that Christians sometimes consider our faith as fire insurance – "Let us put our faith in God, so that when we die, we can be sure we'll go to heaven and not hell". Again, this feels so far away that it is hardly a motivation for us in our everyday ordinariness.

What then is a good reason to centre your life on someone so abstract, yet so powerful? For me, the answer is simple – Relationship! A relationship with a constant, all-powerful, ever-loving friend is the ultimate desire of every human heart.

As humans, we were created to be in relationships and this desire constantly drives us towards forging them whether subtly or overtly, consciously, or unconsciously. Having an established relationship with someone who truly cares matters to us all in more ways than we often acknowledge. To illustrate this further, I will share an experience that I had at a fairly young age.

As someone who was raised in a 'Christian home', my understanding of faith first centred around going to church at least twice a week, not telling lies or using abusive words, and dressing modestly. This was mostly fine until I began to interact with the world at large while attending boarding school.

At this time, I began to face real issues that going to church did not seem capable of solving. I also began to perceive the world from a bigger lens than I could have previously imagined. At this point, faith had to become real and personal to me, or fake and not useful at all. Thankfully, God began to seek me out simultaneously. He helped me understand that He was calling me to a personal relationship with Him, where I could talk with Him and He with me.

I remember one time when I was deeply saddened by a test that I had missed (remember I attended a large secondary school with over a thousand students? Missing a test wasn't completely out of place because there were enough other students in the class for me to go unnoticed). Because I did not feel like anyone could help with this burden, I turned to my often-ignored devotional to read the lesson for the day as a desperate cry for help. Interestingly, that lesson spoke directly to my 10-year-old heart about how God loved me and how He could help me out of any challenging situation.

Even today, I remember how peaceful I felt after I read that lesson. Although the situation was not immediately resolved, the knowledge that God was with me was the anchor I needed to get through that day, and He had found a way to deliver the message to me. I felt absolutely loved and cared for as I realised that I was not alone.

A few days later, by an interesting turn of events, I was able to sit for the test with students from another class. I later learned that the Department had decided to create an opportunity for students who had missed their tests. Luckily, I was at the right place when information about the impromptu timing and location was dispersed. Looking back, I realise that the situation was not such a big deal, but this makes it more precious that God chose to reveal Himself to *little me* through such a mundane event. At the end of that week, it became clear to me that

God was real. This marked the turn where I really began to approach the concept of faith as a relationship with God beyond the rote and routine of religious rituals and church attendance.

All this is to say that faith is not something external to you. Religion may be external to you, but faith is not. Faith provides you the lifetime opportunity of being known by and knowing someone large enough to create the universe through a personal relationship. It offers the privilege to walk alongside a constant friend as you journey through this uncertain world. It gives you a chance to have a Father who can truly be with you and for you wherever you go, no matter what happens. And though this relationship begins as a matter of trust and decision, it is not expected to remain as such.

Because true relationships involve give and take, faith is also an opportunity to give and take.

God gives you his unconditional love and support, and you give Him your attention, trust, and then obedience. Amazingly, this exchange has the potential to make you into the most beautiful version of yourself and help you live out the highest purpose intended for you by the Creator of the Universe. Ultimately, it is a source of satisfaction that compares to nothing else, and I believe it is just what we all are searching for.

> *A commitment to a life of faith also entails trusting God with your life and embracing fellowship with Him and His principles for living every day.*

Faith: Version Twenty-something

I have come a long way from my childhood encounter and though I am still a person of faith, there have been days when this adult life had me wondering if there's a different version that I need to find. As a 10-year-old in boarding school who was beginning to discover a personal faith, most of what I needed to wrap my head around was reading my bible – actually, devotional – everyday, not telling lies (this was particularly difficult because of bullying seniors who seemed out to send me on endless errands), doing my best to go to chapel as often as possible, and generally obeying school rules. As a *twenty-something* though, the demands of faith are more complex and nuanced than I could have imagined when I was committing to this life of following Jesus all those years ago.

Holding fast to your confession of faith in this season involves drawing closer still to your Father God and discovering new dimensions of Him. Acknowledging the constant of His love and care for you and the wisdom of His providence is a great springboard for launching into this discovery. I have found it also important to bear in mind that while your lifetime seems relatively short from the view of eternity; eternity is a long time coming and the pressures of today will look different in time. Having this mindset will provide you a platform from which to engage the demands of this phase without losing your grounding in faith. The following practical tips will help you build on this foundation:

1. Relax, and realise that God is all knowing, and He does have a plan for you.

Do you remember that time in elementary school when you failed a test and cried all the way home? Or came second in a competition and were inconsolable? Maybe this was not you, but it was definitely me. It did not matter what anyone said to me at the time; I was convinced that I was a failure because of those minuscule events. In retrospect, I was clearly wrong. Similarly, as much as this decade constitutes critical years of your life, it is important to realise that your life is really a masterpiece of many different parts that will keep evolving until the end. As such, I encourage you to put pressure on yourself to give every day your best, but also give credence to God for knowing more than what you know. Do not despair based on the results that you see or do not see in the moment, but trust that God is working through all things for your good.

2. Prioritise communion with the Father

At this stage when there are abundant demands vying for your time and attention, it may seem as if there is no space left for God. Yet, this is a good time to structure your life in a manner that creates space for communion, however that works for you. Don't despair when you realise that the routine of times past is lost but make the effort to create new routines at every turn and persevere till you can build again a place of communion with Father-God. While the place may change from time to time – for example, after graduation, or a relocation, or with a new job – the effort should be continuous. Because our faith is based on relationship, not religion,

> *...we must prioritise communion in our lives, lest we find ourselves without our Anchor – not because He left, but because we left Him behind.*

3. Submit your heart to God, and learn courage

As people of faith, a deep desire for many of us is to discover and follow God's will for our lives. In my experience, this desire threatens to paralyse many, when it feels like there is no clear communication of "direction" from God. Being a person of faith does not absolve you of the need to develop courage and confidence in your God-given abilities.

Sometimes God speaks clearly on certain issues, and other times, he gives just enough light for the next step. It is your responsibility to walk the path set before you with courage and grace even when you do not have all the answers you want. God may not always lead in the ways we want, but He will always lead us higher, and we must be able to forge ahead even when we do not have all the details laid out.

4. Extend grace to yourself

Sometimes we fall, and though this is not desirable, we must realise that our mistakes do not define us. What counts the most after a fall is the response to it. While the enemy wants to keep us down with guilt and fear, God offers grace and redemption that will help us get going again if we accept.

The temptation to criticise yourself excessively is something to resist. Rather, choose to see yourself through the eyes of the One who loves you and by Himself makes you worthy. Keep a tender heart that loves God, and make sure to respond to Him always and promptly. No matter how bleak the darkness you find yourself, make sure to recognize His loving voice calling you home to healing and restoration.

5. Learn to trust and obey

Loving God is not something we do in words alone, it requires action. Since God has not left us in the dark as to what love means to Him, we know how exactly to live out our love for Him – by obeying. True obedience, though, is born out of trust.

When we trust that God is working for our good in all situations, we are empowered with the confidence we need to obey Him even when it feels inconvenient. To love God is to keep His commands, and He already let us know that His commandments are not burdensome.[15] Every time we get to a crossroad where there is a tussle between what God wants and what we prefer, we get a chance to demonstrate our love for Him and prove our trust in Him by doing what He wants. Practising this skill helps us to mature and grow faster into the best version of ourselves.

At this point, I invite you to ponder and identify what you believe to be true about the God who made the universe. And then consider how this belief has shaped your life till now. No matter what you find, know that there is a world of good awaiting you behind the curtains of an adventure with God. Like a faithful lover, He has been wooing you through the journey of your life, offering you rest in exchange for the burdens that earthly life often hands you. This is beautifully articulated in the Bible as,

---

[15] *1 John 5:3 - Loving God means keeping his commandments, and his commandments are not burdensome.*

"Come to me, all of you who are weary and carry heavy burdens, and I will give you rest. Take my yoke upon you. Let me teach you, because I am humble and gentle at heart, and you will find rest for your souls. For my yoke is easy to bear, and the burden I give you is light."

MATTHEW 11:28-30

As you journey through life, there will be difficult days, but God is able to carry you through those days and make something good out of them. He is also able to take the most beautiful days and multiply the beauty in them, because He loves you that much! Today is a good day to lean on and receive His love. Just ask Him to come into your heart and He will. If you already did, now commit to building your relationship with Him for as long as you live.

"Don't let the excitement of youth cause you to forget your Creator. Honour him in your youth before you grow old and say, 'Life is not pleasant anymore.'"

ECCLESIASTES 12:1

Personal Reflection Questions

1. *What do you think is the deepest longing of your heart?*

2. *What does being a 'person of faith' mean to you?*

3. *If you were to choose a solid anchor for your journey on earth, what or who would you consider sufficient to fill that role?*

4. *What one thing can you do daily or weekly to actively cultivate your relationship with God beginning from today?*

Conclusion

THE BEAUTY OF THE *TWENTY-SOMETHING* YEARS IS that they are a wonderful opportunity to make cornerstone choices, i.e., choices that can set the direction for the decades ahead. With the many factors competing for your time and attention in this season, exercising the power of choice has never been more essential.

It is always a good idea to consider what is at stake before you choose so that you can avoid the many attractions that are not worthy of you. Think about the fact that for everything you say 'yes' to, you're inadvertently saying 'no' to something else – at least at the same time. This is a helpful decision-making paradigm.

As you incorporate these learnings into the way you live, remember that every decision you make matters, but no single decision makes you. What this means is that while it is important to do your best to choose wisely every single time, you must learn to extend grace and forgive yourself when you make wrong choices. Inquire to see what factors predisposed you to your mistake, distil the lessons from the experience, and then move on – literally.

Finally, as you contemplate choices, know that there are certain choices you should make beforehand, and then every day. Some examples are:

✓ Choose to show up as often as you can.

✓ Choose to care for your own soul and body.

✓ Choose to prioritise your growth.

✓ Choose to give life your best shot

✓ Choose to try – even if you fail – and choose to get back up when you fall.

✓ Choose to be a ray of light in a world that can get really dark, and to be a sound of hope when things get bleak.

✓ Choose to walk your journey with your head held high and to do your best with all that you have been given.

As I reflect on all I have learned as a *twenty-something*, my learning has culminated into an overall choice for the months I have left in this decade and the decades ahead.

This choice is summed up in my adaptation of a quote by Etienne de Grellet:

> *"I shall pass this way but once; so, let me live to the fullest today. Let me not despair nor hold back, for I shall not pass this way again."*[16]

I hope these words inspire you every day as you set out to live an amazing third decade and more to come on earth!

---

[16] *"I shall pass this way but once; any good that I can do or any kindness I can show to any human being; let me do it now. Let me not defer nor neglect it, for I shall not pass this way again." - Etienne de Grellet*

Epilogue

A FEW WEEKS TO MY 29TH BIRTHDAY, I MADE A spontaneous decision to finally release this book. Having worked on it on-and-off for 3 years, I sensed that it was the right time to let it move on and serve its purpose in the world. I'm proud of you for journeying with me to the end, and I really hope you enjoyed the ride.

Now that you've centred yourself with this compass, I would love to hear about how things go. You can reach me at okezi.ob@gmail.com to share your own *twenty-something* puzzles and victories.

You can also keep in touch via *okeziob.com* where I share reflections and stories that help you make a positive sense of the world. You've got what it takes to thrive through this decade and beyond, so soar high and be all that you can!

Acknowledgments

I T IS NOT EASY TO ACCOMPLISH A BOOK WRITING PROJECT, and certainly not a one-person task. I've had abundant help along the way and would like to appreciate everyone whose direct and indirect investments helped me complete this book, a few of whom I've listed here:

To my Parents – Thank you for always letting me soar and for being the wind beneath my wings. No matter what I come up with, you support me, and then you invest in it. I am committed to gaining great returns for your investments and making you proud, always.

To my Siblings – It's beautiful to see what our relationship has metamorphosed into over the years. Thank you for being a safe place to ask all manner of questions and for your honest reviews and unfiltered feedback.

Majiri, Kome and Marero – It was easy to write this when I thought of you, especially knowing that you would let me know if I wasn't making sense. Thank you for the opportunity to be both your Big Sis and friend.

Joy Oseto Odia – Thank you for reading my first draft in its most embarrassing state and providing both resounding encouragement and detailed critique like only a dear friend can. It's interesting that we ended up with your initial title suggestion despite a pushback that seemed final. Thank you for also holding me accountable to my first and most significant deadline.

Miriam Nji – Thank you for your comprehensive review and kind feedback. Thank you for cheering me on with this project and everything else.

Darling Light Bearers – Thank you for being my friends and sisters, purpose and prayer partners, my bus-stop for vulnerability, encouragement, radical candour, and unflinching support.

My Adopted Sisters – I'm grateful that med school gave me lifetime friends in all 9 of you. Thank you for always being a part of my story.

Oluwatoyin Bankole – Thank you for believing in me. I can't forget that Monday night when you preached my own gospel to me and helped me figure out the fear that was holding me back. You know I love you!

Lolade Olakulehin – Thank you for your review and practical advice on improving the initial manuscript. I appreciate you!

Funmi Okonta – Thank you for the cover designs, long calls, and constant encouragement. You are a very special friend.

Laju Iren – Thank you for kindly affirming my writing skill and the subject of this book. You gave feedback that only a professional could and saved my readers from what could have been a thesis reading experience. I'm still a work in progress on this, but I'm glad you helped me realise.

Adenike Tokan-Lawal – Thank you for your thorough review and honest feedback which gave me the final push to get this done. Despite your busy schedule, you came up with a genius strategy that carried me through my final look over. I am grateful for you.

Seun David-Olurinde – Thank you for being the final bridge between my often-revised, severally edited, complete-yet-sitting-in-my-computer manuscript and my readers.

Foluso Gbadamosi – Thank you for showing me what strengths I had even when I could not see any. Knowing my superpowers has been a game changer for me, and I'll always be grateful to you for walking with me on that journey. Thank you also for doing the honour of introducing my readers to the book experience despite an extremely short notice.

Debola Deji-Kurunmi – I count myself blessed to be a part of your tribe. Thank you specially for the Immerse 30-Day Transformation Course (9th cycle) which sowed a seed in my heart in the middle of a dark season. Just by living your life, you show an example of endless possibilities and I'm grateful to be able to learn progressively.

Mrs. Olajumoke Adenowo – Thank you for your selfless investments to raise a generation of transformational leaders. Thank you especially for Voice of Change which interrupted my regular programming and re-engineered my mindset during very uncertain times in a global pandemic. Your legacy continually inspires me to become more so I can do more for the world.

To the Children I've taught over the years – Thank you for granting me access to your hearts and allowing me love and serve you when our paths crossed. As you grow into adults, I hope that some of the things we learnt help you stay anchored, and if you happen to come across this book, I pray the wisdom it shares makes your journey much easier.

To Father God – Thank You for being my All in all, and for never giving up on me. Thank you for the constant push to be more, gentle reassurance when I doubt, quiet rebuke when I stall, providential opportunities to move me forward, and the gift of life which I do not take for granted. This – like everything else I stretch myself to do – is for You!

About the Book

"A*DULTING IS A SCAM!"* – THIS WAS A POPULAR SAYING among friends and colleagues that started right after our graduation from the university. We were glad that school was over, however, the 'real world' looked nothing like we had imagined. As realization dawned, we found that we did not feel ready to take on this new season of life.

As a young person 'arriving' at adulting, I imagine that you can identify with these feelings. *Being 20-Something* shares wisdom that will help you purposefully navigate this phase while maximizing your journey.

Through seven significant themes, the book sets a preparatory foundation and creates room for important personal reflections that offer a shoulder to stand on. Its practical guidance will position you, dear reader, to thrive in this season and beyond.

About the Author

OKEZI OBRUTU IS A MEDICAL DOCTOR AND RESEARCHER who is passionate about raising a confident, competent, resilient, and legacy-minded generation. She invests in children through various platforms including a foundation that provides exceptional learning experiences to children in underserved communities.

Her deepest desire is for people to know how much they are loved by God and to see this knowledge empower them to flourish despite life's ups and downs. When not at work, you can find her reading, writing, or enjoying the beauty of nature.

www.ingramcontent.com/pod-product-compliance
Lightning Source LLC
Chambersburg PA
CBHW071758150726
47998CB00005B/1989